"EXPERIENCE A WALK TO REMEMBER"

WITH GOD'S HAND OVER MY LIFE

Based on a True Story

Written by Bianca McClain Miller

xulon PRESS

Copyright © 2011 by Bianca McClain Miller

"Experience A Walk To Remember"
With God's Hand Over My Life
by Bianca McClain Miller

Printed in the United States of America

ISBN 9781612159119

All rights reserved solely by the author. The author guarantees all contents are original and do not infringe upon the legal rights of any other person or work. No part of this book may be reproduced in any form without the permission of the author. The views expressed in this book are not necessarily those of the publisher.

Unless otherwise indicated, Bible quotations are taken from The New International Version (NIV) of the Bible. Copyright © 1981 by Rainbow Studies, Inc.

www.xulonpress.com

INTRODUCTION

As I share this true story, my greatest desire is that you experience and relive every memory with me. I hope that my words can express the true reality of this experience and the challenges, since today all they are…memories.

Having changed the actual names for privacy.

Psalm 139:23, 24
Search me, O God, and know my heart; test me and know my anxious thoughts. See if there is any offensive way in me, and lead me in the everlasting way.

DEDICATION

I dedicate this book to my Lord and Savior Jesus Christ. I give God Almighty all the Glory for all He has done and will continue to do in my life. Also for the many lives that will be touched through this book. To God be all the Glory!

CONTENTS

Introduction v
Dedication vii

Chapter 1.- Birth in Mexico & Move To Australia 11
Chapter 2.- Move Back to Mexico 16
Chapter 3.- Trip to The USA 21
Chapter 4.- Living in New Mexico 23
    A Divorce
Chapter 5.- Living in San Marcos Texas 27
Chapter 6.- Bye, Bye Texas, Back to NM 29
Chapter 7.- God Is Real In My Life! 33
Chapter 8.- God's Divine Protection Over Me! 37
Chapter 9.- A Great Blessing in My Life 41
Chapter 10.-A Few Challenges to Face 46
    A Faithful Tither
Chapter 11.-God's Favor in Our Lives 56
Chapter 12.-Mom Needs a Liver Transplant 62

Author's Biography 67
Back Cover

Chapter 1

Birth in Mexico & Move To Australia

Born to an American Father and a Mexican Mother in 1964. With that said, I must recall a weird start, my grandmother had given birth to my youngest uncle, that makes him to be 3 days older than me, as she checked out of the San Jorge Hospital in Durango Mexico, my Mom Flor Larios de McClain checked in the very same room, and there I was, born on October 23rd 1964…leave it to no imagination on my parents behalf, to name me as Mother Flor McClain Larios, what a name.

My Older brother Mac the IV, with a nickname of Junior, was 1 year older than me. As we grew up, he named me Bianca. I am grateful to Him for that. When I turned 1 year old, my parents decided to move to Australia, since my Father, Grandfather and uncle Phillip went on a venture and bought land for ranching and buffalo hunting near the Ropper River, called Sun Bidgen, close to where Crocodile Dundee was filmed, so you may have an idea of the territory, out in nowhere land.

"Experience A Walk To Remember"

Junior and I rode our dogs as horses and swam with the crocs, needless to say we survived. Our Mother knew no English when we moved to Australia, the only means of communication at the ranch also called station, Sun Bidgen, it was the radio. The closest town and also clinic, was about 230 miles to a town called Catheran. I remember Junior and I hiding in a barrel at the clinic so that we wouldn't get our shots.

3 Years later my sister Vanessa was born, WOW! There were 3 of us now, Junior and I were closer than peanut butter and jelly, we went everywhere together and did everything together as well. Now we wondered how this was going to be, with a baby.

One night Junior and I stayed up waiting for Dad to arrive from a long trip, wondering if He brought us something back. So at about 2am Dad came in, we hugged Him and holding onto His legs waiting to hear what he brought us…come on outside with me and I will show you two what I brought you…we were so excited, we followed Him out and on to the corrals we went, from the trailer He unloaded 2 baby calves, We were the happiest kids that early morning.

WOW! They were WILD! Bucking and Kicking all the time, it was very exciting to have, of course we tried riding them, but was not possible. Most of the time Junior and I would end up climbing up a tree and wait for them to lay down, and then we would make a dash to the door. So Mom would have to encounter the calves and feed them for us, we would watch her and laugh as they would chase her around and buck her.

I remember going for a swim with Mom, Junior and a little boy that was visiting, there we were splish, splash and all of the sudden Mom says Ups! You better get out because there is a crocodile coming, so we looked, he was about 10ft away, can we stay longer since he is not that close?...and she dragged us out, so there was Mr. Croc staring at us, probably missing lunch, or thinking we could have been a great snack! Ha, ha, ha. I ask Mother now, what were you thinking, taking 3 toddlers to swim in crocodile infested waters ? She said…I guess I wasn't thinking, I was so naive and it was so hot. All I know is that it was God's Divine Protection over all of us. So here we are.

The Ranchers would call each other for reports or to advise of someone coming our way, always expecting hospitality, since that was the thing to do, so Mom got a dictionary and between all the neighbor ranchers on the radio she was able to learn English, they were all very kind and patient with her, until she learned.

Well is time for Junior and I to attend school, pre-school and kinder garden, Junior is 5 and I am 4years old. So we moved to Darwin, and I remember my first day of school, I stayed glued to the bench outside my classroom and cried all day. I was so glad to see my Mom when she picked us up. I finally learned to stay and know it would be okay. Junior would go check on me at break and that made it better.

"Experience A Walk To Remember"

There was a sack lunch I always hoped for the little chocolate milk and the little bag of cheetos, that was the highlight of my school day, it was like a surprise, when you open the sack you find out what you got, plain milk or chocolate. There was a much taller and bigger girl than me, she was an aborigen girl that started picking on me, I couldn't understand why she didn't like me, because at the ranch we had an aborigen family that lived and worked with us, so the kids, Junior and I would play together and we liked each other always. But here was this tall and big girl, taking my chocolate milk and my bag of cheetos, so I would run at lunch and look for Junior, if I couldn't find him, she would have my lunch. So pre-school was not my favorite place to be.

Sometimes Junior and I would walk home from school, as we walked through a certain street, there were these boys that would chase us and throw rocks at us, they were much older than us. One day we were walking by that street and we saw only 1 kid there, so Junior said to me, let's go over and I will hold him and you bite him and we run!...so that we did, but as we kept running, we ended by the beach and Junior found a watch, so we kept walking, looking for a watch for me, how sweet! Well it got dark and no watch for me yet, then we see the police cars coming and we knew we were in big trouble for biting the boy, not because our parents were searching for us. So either way we were in big trouble.

Later that month we were sneaking in the kitchen, my brother holding a stool and me on it, getting the flint stones vitamins from on top of the fridge, so we could have one more without Mom knowing, as I reached for the bottle, the door bell rings and a knock on the door, so Mom walks by us and Busted! was the word. A Police officer asking questions about the neighbor's house next door, someone had broken in, did we know anything about it?... so we said yes, these big boys had asked Junior to jump the fence and open the door from the inside, so he did and left. Mr. Police Officer had a serious talk with us and we were in Huge trouble, no friends over, no playing outside, no swimming...for I don't know how long, was a long month thou.

My Parents had made friends with a Greek couple, they loved for Junior and I to go visit, the lady would make us peanut butter and jelly sandwich, they were delicious to us, not being a food staple in our home. But Mom had to ask her to stop feeding us PB & J's anymore, because we had gained weight that summer.

Chapter 2

Move Back to Mexico

Well in 1970 we moved back to Durango Mexico and behold our Mexican mother had forgotten to teach us Spanish, so we couldn't communicate in school, so we had to learn Spanish and miss 1 year of school. Then we manage to neglect our English and all we spoke was Spanish. Then we moved to the coast, Puerto Vallarta, Jalisco, were there are a lot of Americans and Canadians residing there, as it is a turist place. So there we were again, taking English this time, we had tutor classes twice a week for English and we got to practice with the turist and family when possible.

My Father bought a meat market, to cater to the hotels and restaurants in the area, specializing in American cuts. It was a great business. At the time there were 11 hotels and about 8 nice restaurants and plenty of locals.

Puerto Vallarta has great vegetation, mangoes, coconuts, plums, tamarinds, 3 or 4 different kinds of bananas, jicama, guanabanas, sugar canes, pineapples, papaya, oranges, tangerines, avocados, etc. We grew

"Experience A Walk To Remember"

up eating these delicious fruits in abundance, absolutely refreshing. We would get out from school around 2pm, and outside the school, you could buy different kinds of fruit slices or bags of chopped fruit with lime juice, salt and chile powder, or just by itself. Just what the doctor ordered. It was hot and humid, that would refresh us.

We attended Colegio Ninos Heroes, it was a catholic school run by nuns. When time came for junior high, school hours were in the evening, 5pm to 9 pm.

We lived across from the beach once for a few years, so we would spend our evenings and weekends at the beach, people watching, boogie boarding, catching baby crabs, buring ourselves in the sand, playing volleyball in the pool, anything close to the water since it was hot and humid. We had great times and lot's of memories. We grew up with no TV or Phones at home, parents choice, so we had no choice but to be outdoors and take full advantage of our energy. So sometimes we would spend the day riding our bikes to our friend's ranch, it would take us all day there and back, on the way there we would eat fruits from the trees on the side of the road. Our friend's ranch had cows, so if we get there at the right time, we could milk the cows or just watch. We had good grades in school, A's and B's, except for my sister Vanessa, always in honor roll miss smarty pants. Even now in her early 40's she has decided to go back to school and all A's, very few B's, almost none. She would lose sleep over a B.

I finally got to go to a public school for my 7th and 8th grades. I couldn't wait to attend that school. For my shop class I decided to take electricity, so there I was wiring a lamp and POP! Kick the breaker and lost power for over 1 hour, I don't know exactly what happened, but that was my first and last week in that class. I did good in the volleyball team, also we had a dance team for opening games at the stadium, I really enjoyed that, well that lasted about 5 games over weekends, since some girls had been murdered with an ice pick at the stadium over a period of weekends, so I was no longer allowed to participate in this activity for safety reasons.

We would go camping at the beach over the weekends at least once a month and in the summer, my Dad, and 2 or 3 other couples with their children and our friends, 3 guys and 2 of their sisters plus the 3 of us. There were enough of us to make it fun and be able to play volleyball in the water. We were not afraid of sharks, just went around them or move over to the side, so here we were at Punta de Mita, which is at the end of the bay, all the youth is playing volleyball in the water, and we are up to the chest and waist on water levels, since some of us are shorter, well here came my uncle and told us to get out there was a shark coming our way, he was about 10ft away, so we waited for him to be much closer before we got out, it really was no big deal, …but that summer the movie JAWS came to PV to the theaters near us, let me tell you after we all watched it …the water didn't look so great after that, so we all became very cautious about getting in the ocean and were, the movie took away a lot of fun from us. It didn't stop us from exploring thou, but the swimming goals and challenges were gone, we used to dare each other to play

"Experience A Walk To Remember"

dead, that meant to float on the water and let the current take you as far as possible...can you imagine that?...Jaws would have been a happy camper with us.

The natives of PV are very friendly people and very simple, always catering to the turist. We lived in Puerto Vallarta for 9 years.

There was a boy I had a crush on, he was a year older, He was in Junior's class. I wasn't allowed to date yet, but that didn't stop me from trying. My sister was a trouble maker, always bribing me so that she would not tell my parents I liked this boy. Well she said enough to my Mom one Sunday, that Mom decided to send me to Durango to my grandma's for the summer, once there, I decided to get a perm, it looked so cool on other girls, I wanted one bad, but first let me tell you about my hair, it is very fine and soft, so after the perm it looked like an afro, no kidding, I couldn't do one single thing with it, not even a pony tail, every morning I begged my hair to grow, I wore a handkerchief for the rest of the summer,....so my summer was the worst that year.

I was so glad to be back home and ready for school to start, I am almost 14years old and making new friends, I liked all my classes, and that boy was still in the picture. I knew I could make a date possible somehow, someday, but meanwhile we send each other notes and meet down the hall or at recess for maybe 5 minutes, we were both so nervous about speaking, so we had almost no conversations, I think we were tongue tied...it was so silly.

"Experience A Walk To Remember"

At this time Junior decides to part our close relationship, we were like peanut butter and jelly since little, great partners in crime, and now I am on the way for him to pick up on girls, since some girls think I am his girlfriend, others would ask. So one day he decides we need to have a serious talk, he tells me we can no longer hang out together, I need my own friends and he needs his own as well, we can go to places as a group, but not just him and I as always.

WOW! That was hurtful, I couldn't understand why he would push me away just like that, so I cried, I didn't know how to handle such rejection, that was my best friend and so used to being around him. I tried sneaking around and accidently ending up at the same places, etc. So finally I became friends of his friend's sisters and that made it better for me, and everyone was happy. That was truly hard thing to process, but very normal and understandable.

In Mexico when you turn 15 years old, they have a party called Quinceanera, that is like presenting you as a young woman, so it was my time to get excited and know I would be having a huge party for my 15th B-Day, even thou I am not 14 yet, but it gave me lots of time for planning and adding people to my guest list.

Well my Parents had a classic car, a 1943 Ford Coupe, we had to push to get started and the trunk opened for seating, with a very unique horn and sound, it was a novelty when out in town, so an American couple, car collectors from Pueblo Colorado wanted to buy it badly, so my Parents sold it, the deal was for us to deliver it to them and that was a great excuse to make a trip to the USA.

Chapter 3

A Trip To The USA

At that time some close friends of the family and also my Dad's youngest sister and family lived in New Mexico in the mountains, which is on the way to Pueblo Colorado, so it was a great reason for delivering the car. We could stop by and visit friends and family on the way back.

So we traveled from Puerto Vallarta to Pueblo Colorado, once in the mountains, we loved it, the feel, the smell, everything about it. We delivered the car and stayed overnight and head back to New Mexico the next day, were we spent a week at my aunts, exploring the area, absolutely beautiful and almost no people, maybe 200 residents at the time. So my Parents bought a house that was under construction and they would need to return in 6 months for finishing touches, etc. Hoping that in that time they could sell our home, business and small ranch in PV…WOW! Moving? What about our new friends? We just made new ones, we are attending the school we always wanted to go to, this place is beautiful, but we don't really want to move, either way it was a done deal, once school year is over to New Mexico we go.

So there went my plans for my Quinceanera party…and of course I thought I was in love with this boy, later a lady told me that is what you call puppy love dear.

Chapter 4

Living in New Mexico

A Divorce

Well I was so upset about the move, I decided to stay in my room most of the summer and listen to sad songs, like airsupply, etc. I was almost 14 years old.

We had to take a school bus ride of 45 minutes there and 45 minutes back, since the school was in a different town. But the nice thing was that we only attended school 4 days out of the week. In the winter months we could ski Saturday, Sunday and Monday, that was pretty cool for us. For our first year in NM, we had 2 house guests, one my age and one Juniors age, they were attending school with us so that their English would be better, so we all had a great winter that first year. Every so often we did have school on a Monday, only to make up a snowy day, but not too often. We would be at the ski area at 8:30 am, on time for the lifts to open at 9 am until the last run of the day at 4:30 pm. We enjoyed every minute of the day.

That was my freshman year, it was hard for me, I had a teacher that talked with his glasses on his mouth, the whole class, so I never understood a word, I would study the text book and hope for the best at test time, it was science. I barely passed the class, I think he felt sorry for me, I did, I felt clueless the whole time, so a C I got. The rest of my classes I did A's and B's.

In the summer my brother Junior got a job at the golf course, and he became a pretty good golfer, so he got a scholarship for New Mexico Military Institute, so that left me to continue school by myself. My Parents decided to send me back to Mexico to Durango to my Grandma's for the school year, at a girl's school run by nuns (again). But this time it was different, my Grandmother had traveled to Europe and stayed 3 months gone, so it was my aunt 3 years older than me and my uncle, the same age as me. There we were on our own. A friend and I started ditching school to go to her sister's house to visit, have coffee and eat cookies, so meanwhile she would smoke like a train, she just didn't like school, but the problem was that it started affecting my grades, I had to make up one class over a weekend they call those having to take an extra ordinary test, she was use to that, but I wasn't. All she wanted to do was smoke, she was raised by her younger brother that was 10years older than her, since her parents had died when she was 9 years old, he was very strict and over protective, that making her want to smoke even more. I think she is a few years older than me, until this day she won't tell me so that means she didn't pass a few years…Oh well.

"Experience A Walk To Remember"

My aunt and uncle had a surprise party for my 16th B-Day, the lady across the street was an attorney and had two little girls I would teach English twice a week, so she made my cake, a Beautiful 4 layer cake from scratch, almond and Chantilly frosting, it was Delicious! There were about 35 people, it was a blast! Sweet 16 away from home.

When the school year was over I went home back to the mountains. I had a good summer and had started a job at the convenience store in town, I would go in the evenings and stock up the coolers, also I would babysit for a few couples every so often.

Well my Parents are getting a divorce and they are fighting over custody of the children, by then I had 2 little brothers, Lee that was 5 and Alonso a baby, so Mom decides to stay until the house sells and Dad is moving back to PV, with all of us, except for Junior, since he is attending first year in college in San Marcos Texas. Mom says I will come for you and the kids once the house sells. So to PV we go. There my Dad met a new friend, she was from Houston Texas, an attorney and she had a daughter that was about 2 years younger than Vanessa, so they both got along great and spent a lot of time together, this allowing my Dad's friendship to get closer. Vanessa was almost 14 and I was almost 17 years old. Meanwhile my Dad received a phone call from his stepmother in San Marcos Texas, were my grandfather was living. There had been an accident and my grandfather had lost his life, so the funeral would be in a few days. What happened was my grandfather and my Dad's half brother 12 at

"Experience A Walk To Remember"

the time, as they were driving on a pickup, a big semi was coming their way and towards my uncle, so grandfather moved the truck to make it hit his side and save my uncles life, otherwise he would still had lived many more years, he was 72 years old at the time, very healthy, he would do 100 pushups and sit ups every single morning. He was a pipe smoker, always wore cowboy boots, and a distinguished cowboy hat, that is how I remembered him, even when he go visit at the beach, never wore shorts, he sit there and watch the waves while he smoked his pipe.

Chapter 5

Living In Texas

So, of we went to the funeral in San Marcos Texas. We ended up staying there for almost a year. Junior was attending the college there in San Marcos, my Grandfather had offer to pay for his schooling since he was the first to want to study medicine and become a doctor like his father had been, So with great joy he wanted to put Junior through school. After His death, things changed, my step grandmother and an uncle had paid the lawyers to change the will according to their plans, leaving Junior with no more help, so Junior decides to finish the semester.

I was able to get a job at an oyster bar, it only lasted 2 weeks, until they realized I was not 18 yet. Oh well! I applied at a Chinese restaurant, got to work 2 days, the owners and staff, none of them spoke English, so I knew no Chinese either, could not communicate even once. Junior and I opened a little taco stand on an intersection between Martindale and San Marcos, on the weekends, we did okay, but mostly had fun cooking and eating.

"Experience A Walk To Remember"

My Dad's lady friend would come visit over the weekends a couple of times per month, she really liked us and became part of the family, so kind and caring. But when Mom found out about her, she flew to San Marcos the very next weekend. She made my sister and I box every gift she had given us and mail it back to her asap. That being one of the hardest things I've ever done, once at the airport, she made me call her and tell her we wanted nothing from her and stay away from us, Mother standing by me telling me every word I must say, me crying and having to repeat all those awful things to someone that had been so kind and caring when we needed the most, very hard thing to do. Somehow she knew we were made to do that, as I was talking with her on the phone, she told me not to worry, she knew my mom was telling me to do that, am glad, because that made me feel 10% better, but was unbearable for me to do. I flew back to NM to help my mom pack, since the house had sold and she was planning on moving to San Marcos and make things work, put the pieces back together. Once we got back to Texas, our Parents decided for all of us to go through counseling as a family. The counseling sessions were not a good thing, we would end up in arguments on the way home, making things worse, the counselor advised us to attend a charismatic church, but we didn't understand what they were talking about, since we were catholic, so we stop going. The truth we didn't want to become a family like before.

Chapter 6

Bye, Bye San Marcos, Back to New Mexico

So now Junior, Vanessa and I decide to leave Texas and come back to the mountains, so New Mexico here we come! I was almost 18 years old, Vanessa almost 15, so she can only visit for a few months and then go back home and school, but Junior and I got jobs at the ski area ahead of time, He is to work ski patrol and me at children's ski school. We also waited tables at night, so we moved in to a condo that was walking distance from work and split the bills, so that is when we started partying, after work. I had previously dated a guy that was 20 years old and me not even 18 yet, by me being 17 that was not a good idea, but parents seem to be okay I guess, they never said anything against it. They knew his parents, so assumed he was ok, but the truth he was a druggie and became abnoxious when drunk. Before my parents divorced, we had a party at the house in NM, my boyfriend came over and wanted us to go to a bedroom and there things happened without my consent, I was very intimidated by him and also scared, specially knowing people were outside the room, what if they found out…anyway I thought if we were to marry one day, it would fix it all, so a few months later he gave me an engagement ring, now I was engaged, took some of the guilt away. Then a few months afterwards is when we ended in Texas, my fiancé went to visit a few times. At the time my Dad's lady friend called me one weekend from her home in Houston. She said all excited, some friends of mine and I are having a bridal shower for you, let me pass you the phone, so each lady congratulated me and wish me a great marriage, the next weekend she came to visit and out of her trunk came all my bridal gifts from the shower, each gift nicely wrapped and with a card from those sweet ladies. A crock pot, an electric can opener, a toaster, a toaster oven, a blender, a mixer, silverware, kitchen towels, a coffee maker and a cooking book.

WOW! Someone excited about my wedding finally. She would look over the bride catalogs with me and got excited to give me ideas. She gave me a very expensive ring that had been in her family for 2 generations, but I gave back of course, it just meant a lot to me at the time, because of the way she presented it to me. She had also offered to buy a condo for a wedding gift, but that wasn't going to happen, is too much and the wedding didn't happen anyway. My fiancé came to visit afterwards and took the gift to NM to keep until we marry. Needless to say, out of all those gifts, all I have is the crock pot…where do you think they went? His next girlfriend he decided to move in with, a few months later. Then he married, got divorce and married the sister, had kids with her and divorced her as well and married yet another sister and had kids with her also, how crazy this became, he lives in Utah, but he is not a mormon…this has to be very confusing to the children, the aunt/sister/cousin/1/2sister?...I am truly glad my life was not with him. But the rejection, asking me for the ring back so he could turn around and give to the next victim, with no excuse or reason whatsoever, that was very hurtful. The day I decide to go to his parents to pick up my bridal gifts, there was only one left, the crock pot, what a jerk! That was to be my blessing, not his and who knows who's. Oh well. Life goes on and now I was 18 years old, hopefully not as naive. By the way, I still have the crock pot.

Well I met someone else, Donie, seams nice, kind, polite, likes to party and as time goes by, find out he is a pot head! But we started dating, then when I turned 19 years old my Mom and Aunt Betty invited me to go to Mexico to a women's retreat, at this time my parents had moved back to the mountains in NM, am sure they weren't following us, ha, ha. They had remarried.

I went to the women's retreat and got saved and spirit filled, it was an awesome experience, changed my views on religion as I knew, having been catholic all our lives, were you fear God, so are not allowed to pray to Him, instead have to pray to the virgin Mary and ask her to intercede to God in your behalf, and also pray to all the saints, which I really don't know how many they were… very confusing and mysterious. WOW! How simple and clear things

"Experience A Walk To Remember"

became, full of questions we were. So now life had a meaning to me, and God was someone I could learn to love and know, have a relationship with Him and there was a huge window of opportunity, unknown things for my future. A true hope in my life.

Chapter 7

God Is Real In My Life!

I came back changed, Junior got saved and we would attend a charismatic meeting once a week, the Lord would speak to our hearts through the Bible (The Word). So we decided to attend a Bible school in Tulsa Oklahoma, VBI Victory Bible Institute founded by pastor Billy Joe Daughtery, may He rest in peace. My favorite class was conforming to the image of Christ, I loved that class, couldn't get enough of it. So I went for 3 semesters and then went back home to the mountains. My boyfriend Donie picked me up at the airport in Albuquerque, and so we drove home. He slowly started partying around me, he knew I was trying to stay away from it, but not having a church and any other kind of support, it made it easy for me to fall back into partying, but with such guilt I would go to sleep at night, asking God for forgiveness for messing up over and over, I just wasn't strong enough on my own to change. There were 2 churches in town, a Baptist church and a catholic, I didn't get anything out of either one, I wanted more, in deph, something that felt real, like I had experienced in Tulsa and at that women's retreat in Mexico, were I got saved. I had a hunger for God in my life, I didn't understand how to go about it on my own, what I was to do with my life. I had no sense of direction I should say. When in Texas I looked into becoming a stewardess, but I was 1 inch too short to be considered for the training. The other thing I thought I may like to do was become an interior designer or decorator, but I didn't want to have two years of nothing related to that in college, so I gave up that route.

Well I had a major surprise, I became pregnant, my whole world came to an end, I did about 10 different home test in a week and they were all positive. I really didn't know what to do now. Somehow I felt as thou they were twins, for whatever reason. Donie and I would talk about it and it was no big deal to him, whatever, whenever, I'll be there for you, of course he mention marriage, but I didn't even consider the possibility once, him no steady job and a pot head, not what I want. I went to work at the ski school and talked to a co-worker, told her what was going on, she knew very well about a specific clinic in Santa Fe NM, a 2hr drive for us, a few of our other co-workers had gone there as well as her, that is your only option she said to me and gave me the contact information on the clinic. I cried and miss work for the next 3 days, trying to figure a way out. Abortion is murder, how can I even think of it? They brain wash you, making you think is not murder if done in the first trimester, bla, bla. I am literally scared and afraid of God's punishment over my life if I do this. The final decision is to make the appointment for the procedure, one of the requirements is that you be at least 10 weeks pregnant for the fetus to be big enough so that it could be destroyed, so that meant I had to wait 2 more weeks, so made my appointment and waited for that dreadful day.

I remember it was in February, a very snowy day. We had over 2 feet when Donie picked me up from the condo, and the snow was coming down fast and heavy. I had begged God every day and every night to fix this for me, so I wouldn't have to go through with it. You may wonder why I didn't go to parents for help, but a year before an aunt had a baby out of weddluck, my grandmother disowned her, so that said, it would be me as well in our family, so I just imagined it would be the same. I had such shame anyway. Not a word was spoken between Donie and I on our way to Santa Fe, to the clinic, I couldn't contain the tears coming out of my eyes every second. I was Devastated! Felt helpless and like I was to commit murder and I wanted to die right then and there. I was Begging God to forgive me.

We arrived at the clinic and I told Donie not to come in, wait for me, I would be out when done. It was a waiting room full of adults, no one had a smile on their face, you could feel and smell death, the gloomiest place I had experienced to that day. I registered, was given another pregnancy test and given instructions for ultrasound after the result, so all that is done and in the waiting room I sit, test came out positive, ultrasound showed the image they look for. Meanwhile I can't stop the tears from running down my face, am trying to find hope in the reading materials available in the waiting room, but all I read is about the procedure and contraceptives, etc.

Well it is my turn, I had asked God in silence as I lay on the prep table, please Lord don't let me do this, if you are real save me from this, please! So the doctor proceeds, gets the vacumm in place and nothing came out, he examines me and does another ultrasound again, well there seems to be no fetus and you have wasted my time, next time make sure you are at least 10 weeks pregnant, got very upset and puzzled at the same time, because we had proof of pregnancy and previous ultrasound images…the thing is God answered my desperate prayer for help, so I know that in His hands are or is my unborn child. To Him I give ALL the GLORY and PRAISE for to me this was a miracle that probably saved my life as well. The guilt would have been unbarable. I know my life would have been shorten sooner after. I could feel God's hand over my life after that dreadful day, what an awesome thing He had done for me. HE IS REAL!

Chapter 8

Divine Protection Over My Life!

After some time I tried breaking the tie between Donie and I, the relationship, since we had such ties. He became obsessed with me, he would brake into the condo when my brother was gone, I would be in the shower, come out and there he be watching TV in the living room, I would ask how did you get in? Oh I came in through the balcony, by the way this was a second floor, not good. So until this day I have night lights all over the house, no fear, but like to make sure I see everything and not imagine it.

Donie's parents live in Lubbock Texas, they came up for a visit and I saw his mom at my work, she was telling me how happy she was that Donie had a job at the ski area, I asked her, he does?...so we were both surprised, I told her it was not true, Donie made his parents believe that, so that would make it okay for him to stay in their home and live here. She invited me over for dinner that evening. Donie picked me up and so we have a nice dinner with his parents and brother, I remember everyone had maybe 1 glass of wine with dinner, but that was it. Is time for me to leave, Donie is giving me a ride home, I was living at my parents at the time, he had a small ford ranger truck. We left the home and as a mad man goes off on me about telling his mom that he had no job. I was caught by surprise, he was furious at me. I just told him I wasn't going to lie to his Mom, I told him if he didn't want me to say anything, he should have told me so, I had no idea.

Well he was so upset that he took a turn towards the mountains, off the main road and started describing how he would leave me for dead in the woods and described the way he would kill me as well, no one would ever find my body. So I opened the door to jump out, he manage to pull me in by the hair and I manage to jump out the truck, he got out faster than I did, I don't know how, then he strangled me, I remember I was calling out the name of Jesus and nothing would come out, not a sound, finally I felt my eyes popping out, then I saw the look on his face change, he realized what he was doing, I know it was God, he let go and asked me to forgive him, apologize so many times, there I was trembling, trying to catch my breath, shaking and crying, praying under my breath and in my spirit. Well he said I can't take you home now, I said let's go to the hotel at the resort, to the sports bar and have a drink, thinking to myself, I can use the phone there, or possibly run into someone I know and ask for help, maybe see security, so we go and I excuse myself to go to the bathroom, make a dash to the phones and as I dial, I felt his hand over my shoulder, I knew I couldn't trust you he said to me, let's go. He became very upset again, so we left, I convince him to go to a different place for a drink the tavern, hoping the same, to see someone I know, I was threaten to speak to anyone or else. So yes a close friend is there with his girlfriend, but they are so drunk, it wouldn't matter. Security walks by me and Donie runs to his truck thinking am talking to security, he stays out there for a while, I manage to go outside when he drove away, to use the pay phone, is 2am and I call my parents, wake Junior up, I can barely talk, I am shaking and frighten, all I can say is am at the tavern, can you pick me up?...he said I am on my way. I hide and lean behind the building, Donie continues to drive by, but never saw me out there. I was close enough where I could run in. Junior picks me up and we drive home, I cried all the way and my body shook nonstop, it felt like my body was in some kind of shock. Junior said to me I am here if you like to talk, but if you don't I understand, but please call the pastors across the street and talk to them. So I called them at 3 am and they said for me to come over, I told them everything and they ministered to me, prayed God's divine protection over me and His Peace in my life.

The next day I could barely move, my back was bruised pretty bad and I had sore spots all over, I had no idea how bad it was until then. But I am alive! The next few months were very scary for me, I don't know where Donie is, could he be behind me? Waiting for me after work, stoking me at work, parked across the street watching everyone that comes in contact with me, etc. I had nightmares, felt very unsafe even at my parents. He finally has a restraining order, but he would still get as close as possible, without getting in trouble.

WOW! That was a part of my life I wish I could erase. We are the ones that make our choices in life, so in return pay the consequences, better to be FREE of all bondage and have Peace in our lives. Thank you Lord for Your Mercy over my life, then and now.

Chapter 9

A Great Blessing in My Life!

The next relationship I was in was so wonderful. He was a great guy, 2 years younger than me thou, but we had a great time together, we enjoyed going to church, he wanted to get married, but we didn't. All I have to say is that he was a great blessing in my life and made me feel safe. We dated almost a year.

I met my husband when I was still dating him, but went for it anyway. Allen and I started going out, so one day both guys show up to see me at the same time, I didn't know how to handle it, so I left them talking to each other. Afterwards they both told me I would have to decide one of them not both. It was a very hard decision, but here I am with Allen and in April 2011 we'll be married for 22 years, plus 4 that we dated. What can I say, time flies when you are having fun! Allen has been a great mate, truly loves me from the heart. He cares for me and provides, I call him my sugar daddy for fun, as we all know, no marriage is perfect, so ours on a scale 1-10 I would say 8,but that is okay, if it was perfect, it would be boring. We face our challenges like everyone else, but we put our trust in God and make the best out of things, when things go wrong.

Both our backgrounds are so different, but together we seem to complement each other well. So you know God put us together. I get excited about things easy, I have a passion for life and I am a dreamer, literally a dreamer, always have a project in mind, believing for it to become real, always dreaming for better projects that I should be a part of, etc. I never lose hope, I like to encourage others to believe in their dreams, specialy if God had given them those dreams, I know how to believe and stand, I have that zeal in me, that is what drives me, I call it passion. I am a giver and nothing gives me more pleasure than blessing someone with a gift, a card, a flower, a phone call or just a hug. I love the holidays, because I don't need a reason for giving, people really have a hard time receiving with no reason, but I do understand, because that is me also. Allen is very meticulous on his work, he likes to figure things out mechanically and technically, so don't say the words I can't to him, because he will find a way to show you it can. Very determined, responsible and enjoys life, tries to make the best of it. He Loves the Lord and that to me is gold, because together we can do our best. So thank you again Lord for such a blessing in my life.

You know, Allen use to smoke 2 packs of cigarettes a day before we got married, he tried quitting a few times, got worse, so for our wedding day he asked God to set him free from it and hasn't had 1 single smoke since, the very next day he couldn't stand the smell of others such as his dad smoking, so that was our wedding gift from God. We had a hard time getting married, we went for marriage counseling for 3 months, then it was time to set the date, I would get nervous and wonder what if we get divorce, what if he's not the one, etc. So the pastor would say come back when you have a date. A year later, okay I think am ready, so of to talk with pastor and guess what? You need to do counseling again, you waited too long, so we do again, the same thing would happen, time for a date and I get nervous, so another year goes by and again, different minister, same thing, finally we got our marriage license and blood test done, a preacher from the Baptist church heard us talking about how hard it was to get married, all we wanted was God's blessing, so he offered to marry us, no questions asked, so we plan our wedding in days, called friends from the phone book and had a wedding were over 150 people showed up. We were just glad, because we considered aloping and being married by a judge. But God had other plans. Of course I had always dreamed of a wedding were I made the party favors, appetizers, we did have appetizers and cake, but no party favors or wedding invitations, what I had looked at in the bride catalogs for so many years. Is okay, we have God's blessing and that is all that really matters.

Back to when I am 19 years old, before Mom and I attended the women's retreat in Mexico, she had become very ill, doctors would tell her it was house wife syndrome, it was a nervous breakdown, etc. Finally she had studies done at different hospitals and went to different specialist in Houston, she had cancer in the liver and there was nothing to do for her it was very advanced, doctor after doctor sent her home to die. She was about 43 years old, with baby Alonso at 2 years old and Lee at 7 years old. At the time she believed it was God's will for her to die, and she would glorify Him by it…this being the craziest thing I ever heard, so on Saturday evenings the catholic priest would come by to pray with her and give her communion, assure her that it is God's will that she die. We be present, watch and listen time after time as she is told by the priest, at that time still Catholics, so He represents our hope, it is God's will for you to die, that will glorify Him. After the priest would leave, she would instruct us on how she wanted us to raise the 2 little ones. At the time she was on oxygen 24/7 and only able to drink the juice of a broth made from certain vegetables. She became more fragile every day.

One day my aunt Betty called, my Dad's younger sister, she wanted to talk to mom, so Dad held the phone over her ear and aunt Betty says: Sister in law, what makes you think that it is God's will for you to die?...The word of God says you are to live and not die, and to declare the works of the Lord, so how can you glorify God by dying? That is nothing but a lie.

John 10:10 The thief comes only to steal and kill and destroy; I have come that they may have life, and have it to abundance. NIV

So my aunt contacted some ladies from women's aglow to come minister to her the truth, the ladies came from the next town about a

40 minute drive, the ladies name was Silvia, she was a pastor's wife, from the Assemblies of God, she brought lots of tapes and books, all healing scriptures and speaking life. So now there is hope in her and all of us, we are so eager to hear more and at the same time very puzzled about it, but the days went by and Mom was gaining strength back, getting better and healthier, so finally she was healed, just by hearing the word and confessing it over her life, God delivered her from death by His Mighty Power. So a few months later is when we attended the women's retreat in Mexico.

Chapter 10

A Few Challenges to Face

A Faithful Tither

My husband Allen and I were blessed by having the opportunity to manage some apartment complex and in return pay no rent, this was for a period of 3 years. We use to go rafting in the Rio Grand on the Gorge in Taos NM, this particular time it was only the two of us and our dog Fluffy. There we were enjoying the rapids, water everywhere, Beautiful day. We pulled over for our picnic lunch on top of some rocks, so that we could watch other rafters come down through the rapids, there came a group of 3 rafts, and they were doing silly moves and flipping over, I laughed at them and said to Allen, I can't believe how silly that was, can you?... he said don't be laughing at them, we are still not done, that could be us. Well after lunch, we get back on the raft and off we went to continue our ride, at the very last rapid, called sunset, the raft tiped over and there we went. I got caught under the water in what felt as

"Experience A Walk To Remember"

a suction hole, it was throwing me from one rock to the other, back and forth, I was able to go up for air and it would suck me down as fast as I would go up, as I fought for every breath and holding on to my life jacket that kept slipping out, then I realize is not let me go, I remember seeing 2 kids fishing on the shore to the left of the bank as we went down, I thought to myself, Oh No! I don't want them to see me drawn, so I prayed and ask God for help. All of the sudden I find myself glued to a rock, like a lizard, I am not sliding or moving, but I am alive, right in front of the boys fishing, about 8ft away, in between rocks. Then someone grabs me by the back of the life jacket and pulls me into their boat, then they CPR me, my lungs were filled with water and my body went into shock, once on shore someone made me some hot tea to relax my body.

I saw my dog running back and forth, not knowing what had happened and Allen was glad to see me, since they went down stream with the raft, there was no way to go back up or even know what had happened to me. So there is a scripture dear to me since I know the reality and meaning of it in my life for that specific day.

Psalm 18:16 He reached down from on high and took hold of me; he drew me out of deep waters....

Psalm 91:2 I will say of the Lord, "He is my refuge and my fortress, my God, in whom I trust"

Well, Allen and I were faithful tithers and givers, knowing how important the tithe is, it belongs to the Lord, at times we would have to chose, pay this bill or tithes, always chose to tithe, we know God honors that.

Proverbs 3:9 Honor the Lord with your wealth, with the first fruits of all your crops;

We stand on Malachi 3:10, 11 Bring the whole tithe into the storehouse, that there may be food in my house. Test me in this, says the Lord Almighty, "and see if I will not throw open the floodgates of heaven and pour out so much blessing that you will not have room enough to contain. I will prevent pest from devouring your crops, and the vines in your fields will not cast their fruit," says the Lord Almighty.

I had a job offer in the next town, about a 40 minute drive. The job consisted on supervising a gift shop, it was called Southwest Marketplace. It was 1,700 square feet, had a lot of different souveniers, Mexican glassware, paper mache fruits and vegetables, flowers, southwest clothing, southwest jewelry, and t shirts, in a great location, right on the plaza. The owners were relocating and were in the process of moving. They had a daughter who they wanted to hand the store over, but her husband did not approve of it, so she missed out on her blessing because of their conflict of interest. At the time we attended the same foursquare church in that town, this was in 1993. WOW! What an opportunity for me, I love working

"Experience A Walk To Remember"

retail, and hoped to have my own store one day, so I was greatly blessed with the opportunity and the pay was 2,400.00 per month, the most I had ever made in a month, so I was very excited and willing to do my best and enjoy every second of every day! I traveled 40 minutes there and 40 minutes back every day except Sundays, I would pray and believe God could make it possible for me to buy the store, even though I had no money or credit for that matter, I just believed and prayed, didn't mention it to Don and Jenny Wilson. 6 months have gone by and the Wilson's are coming to town to pick up some furniture and check the paper work. So there we were at the store, Allen, Don, Jenny and I, we were praying together and then I felt the Lord's presence so strong, Don was trembling, as he tried speaking what the Lord had put in His heart. He said; we are to sell you this business for 10,000.00. Let me tell you, that was equivalent to 100,000.00 now days, so for my husband Allen and I was only something God could make possible. We all took a few minutes to let the news sink in, we said thank you for listening to God. It is a Great Blessing to us, specialy to me, since it's been my desire to have my own store one day, I enjoy working retail greatly. So they went on to tell us how we could agree on a payment plan making it possible to be throughout a 1 year period. So to God we gave all the Glory.

    The overhead in the store was pretty big, the rent itself was 1,700.00 per month, with a 3 year lease, unbreakable, if it was broken, we were still responsible unless we found someone to take over the lease. Well 1994 was a bad year with turist in that town. Many businesses closed their doors that summer. We didn't even make rent for 3 consecutive months, the peak months, so things became tough. At the same time my husband Allen broke his knee at work, slipped of a ladder at work and had to have ACL replacement, knee surgery. He was off work for 3 months. It became a burden as fast as it had been a blessing. We wondered had we missed God in this?

One day I am at the store, praying and seeking God, wondering what is going on, then a young couple from California, they walked in and as we started talking, they saw I had Christian t shirts and also the music that was playing was Christian music, I think it was Michael W. Smith. The lady said to me; you know I suppose to go skiing today at Taos Ski Valley, that is where we are staying. My husband had planned to come into town and walk around the plaza, look at the different galleries and then we were to meet for dinner. As I was getting ready for my ski day, the Lord put it in my heart to come into town with my husband, so all morning I have been wondering why I was to do that, and now at this very moment, I know, for the last month my husband and I have been praying for you and your husband, not knowing you, but we knew that we were to come to this place one day. So WOW! I could feel God's presence in that place, I knew that was an appointed time. We held hands together and prayed, thanking God for His awesome presence in our lives and for bringing us together for such moment. I shared with them our circumstances and how I wondered if I had missed God. It was refreshing for me what happened that day. I knew that I knew it was all going to be ok in the end. Because if I had any doubts, that day they meant nothing, if God has a complete stranger that is willing to pray and intercede for you, in a different state, and they know nothing of you, but are willing to fight through prayer on your behalf, that tells me God would have found someone some were to do the same if this couple had not. So to Him that believes, all things are possible. I chose to believe. I began having health issues, I started hemorrhaging, it was getting worse, finally I was spending so much time going to doctors, that I wasn't able to work, business was getting worse, no business, no turist in town, so we had to close the store. Still owing the Wilson's 6,000.00, 4 months behind on the rent 6,800.00, a few utility bills. We were hoping the Lord would send someone our way to take over the lease agreement for the rent, otherwise the debt would grow very fast. Everything was put into storage. When I became healthier I had a sale and put flyers out, the wholesale value on fixtures and inventory was at least 75,000.00, but at this time it meant anything to get something so that we could get out of such debt. We received a phone call the morning we decide to have the first day of sale, it's my old boyfriend, and his girlfriend is the gift shop manager at the hotel from the resort, they are remodeling the gift shops and t shirt place, she is interested in some of the southwest fixtures, such as the latilla white pine jewelry cases and 2 other ones that match, with shelves and glass, very neat looking and had been custom made for SMP. Anyway they show up at 10am as said, in 10 minutes we had sold those fixtures for 10,000.00. Thank You Lord! At the time I was feeling pretty weak and overwhelmed, but in my spirit I knew that God would work it out for us somehow. Finally I decided to box all the t shirts and sweat shirts and send them to the Metro Ministries in the Bronx, a ministry for the homeless, women and children and I like to support them as much as I can. It was over 1,200 items, about 6 large boxes, over 400.00 for ups fees, the church was kind enough to take care of the freight as part of their missions. That was a blessing as well. The rest of the things went slowly but surely.

    I wrote a poem to the Lord at the time

"To You My Lord"
You are my Life
In whom I Thrive
You are my Hope
In whom I Grow
My Trust is in You my Lord
With Your Love I can go on
The breeze early in the morning
Is sweet and full of your Peace
Strength I find in the hard times
And Peace that surpasses all understanding though my trials
With Your hand on mine

I can conquer and always come forth with Victory

Oh! My Lord; how I long for You

How I long for Joy

You have given me plenty

And plenty more is in store

How could I ever be worthy of You?

If only I could reach the stars

For my hand would be closer to thee.

Written in april 15th 1995

What a blessing. But we still owe the Wilson's, one day as my husband is mowing the lawn, the phone rings and it's the Wilson's, is Don, I was nervous, I knew he would ask for money, what was I to tell Him, feeling like a failure and how can there be an okay answer for owing that money after their generosity, well obedience I should say, but in the natural you try to think what to say, how to make it okay. He said; Jenny and I need to release you from the debt so that you may get well, the last thing you need is a burden in your life at this time, so you are released from the debt, I was speechless, literally, so I called my husband and gave him the phone, as Don went to repeat the same word to him, so debt free we were! In 1 day. We know that being faithful tithers has been the key to all this. We never gave up, at times we grow weary and tired, but never gave up, we knew that with God all things are possible to him that believes, and we believe!

Matt: 21:22 If you believe, you will receive whatever you ask for in prayer.

At the time you think Christians around you would pray for you, instead of talk about you and how you missed God in your life and walk. Nothing from the actual truth, but I choose to be different and God has given me a spirit of humility, always looking for peoples best, and encouraging them at their hardest times, not judging at all, because only God knows what you are facing, and He will never allow you more than you can handle. Maybe things like this is the reason why a complete stranger will pray for you, maybe never get to meet you, but God has people praying for His children when in need, of that you can be assured.

Well as am writing this book, the Lord just reminded me, that before we closed the store completely, the neighbor from the business next door, came by and made us an offer to purchase the inventory and fixtures for 25,000.00, the truth I have no idea why we didn't consider at the time, that would have saved months of stress and the huge burden it was for us, maybe the word is out of ignorance, I take all the blame, but I remember having to go to the store to meet with the business owner and show him the inventory and fixtures that were still in place, I was not feeling well at all, I hope that was the reason, otherwise I do know God had sent us a way out when things got bad soon thereafter, so sorry Lord for not realizing until now what you had done even then, now being 17 years later. God is faithful!

Joshua 1:5b…I will never leave you nor forsake you.

Well some months later a friend of ours had gone into business for herself, things became tough and she found herself on a financial bind, she called one day asking for prayer and to borrow 600.00 or her utilities at the office were going to be shut off. So I had the 600.00 and lend it to her, so time went by and nothing, she wasn't able to pay us back, I told my husband one day, we are to release her from this debt, just as God had done with us for the 6,000.00 months earlier, so we did and the next week my husband received a 1,000.00 unexpected bonus at work. What a blessing!

Chapter 11

God's Favor in Our Lives!

My husband Allen was an electrician and had been working for the same company for 7 years, you need 7 years experience as a journeyman to be able to apply for a contractor's license. The Lord put it in my heart to encourage my husband to get his contractor's license, that meaning to take some classes and test in the big city of Albuquerque, well we had 1,000.00, the course and license fees were about 1,200.00, so of to the city we went and he took the test and was able to get all the licenses required for us to have our own business. We have been in business since 1996, for 15 years. We give God all the glory for every job He sends our way. For the exception of the business logos/info required on the work trucks, and business cards, we do no advertising, with the purpose of letting God have all the glory, there is no reason for anyone to say that we are busy because of this advertising or that one, but because He is the one who has done it for us for the whole time, and our clients come by word of mouth and we also have contractors that choose to work with us because they like our work and honesty. So for His Favor we thank Him every day, we take no job for granted and if we are to bid on a job and not get it, it is okay with us also, we trust that God knows ahead of time which jobs will be benefiting to us and which won't. A year ago when construction had gone to almost none in the area, that was our busiest year yet, so we keep our focus on Him and not what it looks like according to the economy or circumstances around us. We continue to stay faithful to being tithers, we know the Lord honors His word and is true to His promises always.

Matt 18:19-20 "And I tell you more: whenever two of you on earth agree about anything you pray for, it will be done for you by my Father in Heaven. For where 2 or 3 come together in my name, I am there with them.

Allen and I have not been able to have children of our own, I started with female problems ever since we got married, the people around us always feeling sorry for us and telling us things like a marriage is not complete without children, how we are missing out on life, how we will never be a family without kids, etc. We were okay with no children, we wished people would leave us alone about it. Finally we decide to try adopting. Well as most people know, is not an easy process, and if you want to do it through the state, they will have complete control, and pressure you to foster care instead, so that being the case 2 different times, we pull back. So total we tried 7 different times and instances, you go through a roller coaster of emotions, get excited you are going to be a parent, then months go by and all these procedures, and nothing comes of it, then we wait some time and here comes another opportunity and the same roller coaster, it is very emotional and also disappointing when nothing happens. Every time I would change my car, I would choose a different SUV, I needed to make sure there would be plenty of room for all the baby gear, even thou we wanted a toddler(s). My husband would say well we will get the SUV when it happens, but I was trusting it would that year, every year the same since we decided to adopt. I dreaded mother's day. My sweet and kind parents would feel for me and would always bring me flowers and a mother's day card, I kept asking them to please don't do that since I was not a mother, but they would remind me of being a mother to my 3 dogs…is true. What they didn't know is that after they would leave my house I would cry for the rest of the day and throughout the week. Oh well! Is time to change cars, I have decided no adopting, so we got a jeep liberty, from a tahoe to that, very drastic change. Here we were 16 years of marriage and down sized the family car. A lady we know, approached my husband and I after church one Sunday, she said I like you both to pray about adopting a baby, the biological mother is a girl that was our neighbor when we lived in Tulsa, I use to baby sit her until her mother come home from work, so we know them very well, she has asked me to find a Christian home for her unborn child, or the state would put him under foster care as soon as he is born, she was in a place in her life where she could not keep the unborn child, so she has 5 weeks to find a home for her baby and now I ask that you seek God on this, I believe the baby belong with you and your husband. I said thank you so much for thinking about us, but we don't want to adopt anymore, specialy a baby, we are done trying and have closed that door a few years ago, we don't even have a family size car for that reason, I am not baby material anyway. She said, just pray about it and see what God says. Okay we said, I told her I would mention to my sister who lived in Colorado and knew a few people that adopt continually. So of we went and I didn't even want to think about it, just the thought gave me butterflies in my stomach. Well my stomach stayed a knot for the next couple of weeks. She continued to ask what did God say, the mother is waiting for an answer, I would tell her no thank you, and if it is from God He will have to let us know. Finally time for the mother to have final answer, I must call the lady and tell her about my sister's friend that may be interested so I tell Allen am about to call her and what I was to tell her and He looked at me and said "Please say Yes", WOW! He has never talked that way, the sound on His voice was almost desperate, with such hope, I knew that was God's answer, because I had prayed and asked God if that baby was ours, He would show me through Allen, otherwise I didn't want to even consider it. After the answer, I knew that was God's will for us and I accepted the answer then the knot in my stomach was gone, I had so much peace. The fun begins, we need to find an attorney in New Mexico and one in Oklahoma, we need social worker for home studies, if you are familiar with any of this, it takes months, but God took care of every single detail, in a matter of 3 weeks everything required had been done and baby is coming in a week. Before I met with our Attorney in New Mexico, I called the biological mother, I wanted to talk with her and make sure she still wanted to go forth, so she answered and I introduced myself, I told her I was about to meet with our attorney for the first time, but first I wanted to make sure she still wanted to go forward with it, she said; "This baby belongs to you and your husband, I am just carrying him for you" I will not change my mind, he belongs to you and your husband. I speak to him every day and I tell him your Dady's name is Allen and he likes motorcycles, Harley Davidson's, and your Mommy's name is Bianca and she like Betty Boop. That's all I know of you and your husband, and that you are Christians, I just want to make sure he grows up in a home where he will know the Lord. Hearing those words coming out of her mouth, was like hearing God telling me, I did all this just for you! This has been God's gift to us, what an awesome blessing. When the time came the baby was born and we arrived to the hospital 8 hours after, we were with him at the hospital all day and back in the morning again for 3 days until he was released. We have been together ever since, His name is Emmanuel meaning God with us. He will be 5 years old on July 26, 2011. So To God we give All the Glory.

Isaiah 1:19 "If you be willing and obedient, you shall eat the good of the land".

"Experience A Walk To Remember"

My husband and I feel honored to have been trusted by God with our Son, to raise Him and mold Him according to God's perfect will. We trust that the Lord guides us and shows us the way to do this, that He may fear the Lord and come to know Him as His best friend, in that we trust. It has been a challenge at many times, since we had been without children for 16 years, so our personal relationship felt the change, I am just starting to feel as things are a little more normal, but I am so pleased to have Him in our lives and wouldn't change it for the world. It is truly God's greatest gift to my husband and I. We speak divine protection over His life and Godly order over Him spirit, soul and body, every morning, we cover him with the blood of Jesus and speaking blessings over Him and God's favor before Him and behind Him.

Psalm 86:11-13 Teach me, Lord, what you want me to do, and I will obey you faithfully; teach me to serve you with complete devotion. I will praise you with all my heart, O Lord my God; I will proclaim your greatness forever. How great is your constant love for me! You have saved me from the grave itself.

Chapter 12

Mom Needs a Liver Transplant

My Mom is 70 years now, 7 years ago she became very ill again, after 18 years of having been healed. It came slowly, she started having symptoms liver and gallbladder related, more often and she would go see the doctor, he would recommend she see a specialist, but she would go her way and trust it all be okay again, not realizing that at that early stage she could still do things to have symptoms reverse, I truly believe it was God letting her know on time, that something had to be done with medicine, at the time, so like before for being ignorant to God's warnings, we can miss His blessings. This I see now by looking back at the circumstances and how it all happened before and then.

One day she fainted, blood came out and gone she was, it looked like life had left her body, we prayed life into her and clean the mess, it shook us all, a weird experience, we knew nothing of. That night the Lord had me praying and interceding, pacing back and forth, not knowing what was to come. At 7am my Dad calls and tells me he need to take my Mom into the hospital, she was not doing good, so the drive was a 2hr drive to Los Alamos, were her doctor is,, she is in the front on the passenger's side with her nice pj's and oxygen mask on, fighting for every breath she took, almost un-conscience. I sat on the back of the driver's seat, so I could keep an eye on her, and dad drove. I prayed in the spirit and hoped for the best, we knew there was an urgency to her being at the hospital, on the way we would pass 2 different hospitals that she would not even consider, since she is very particular about everything, so there we were, first town, can we take you here?..NO! she said. Keep driving, next town can we go to this hospital please?...No! she said. Well we turn to take the road towards the town we are headed to and I saw her have a convulsion, and she had blood all over her face, I tell Dad pull over she's chocking in her blood, so as soon as he could he did, the next 15 minutes felt like hours, I ran to her side and open the door, my Dad did likewise, she is completely stiff, her eyes are open and stiff, no life in her, no pulse, my Dad steps back and says Sweetie, No, Oh No!, I grabbed his hand and laid it on her and I laid hands on her and I said Dad No!, is not over! I said to her in a firm and determined voice "You will live and Not Die and You will declare the works of the Lord", I speak life to every cell and every organ of your body right now in the name of Jesus! I say Life In Jesus name!...Her eyes moved and she had a pulse, so the Dad started to clean the blood off her face as much as possible, my cell phone had no reception in that spot, so I started waving vehicles going by to stop, nobody would, I finally looked up to heaven and said Lord do something ! The very next truck pulled over, I ask for help, told them I had no reception, they called 911 for us and they took one look at my Mom and stepped back, I told them she had a vein burst in her and had choked on it, but then police arrives, then ambulance, Dad and I talk and nobody listens, they actually interrogated us, well the truth it looked like she had been shot, so they had to make sure am sure…the hospital was 5 minutes away, and as she arrived they started a blood transfusion. Her doctor was contacted in the next town and was waiting for her to be transported there right after the transfusion. What a day, I was going on adrenaline for the next 6 months, I could get my body to slow down, when it finally did, I wasn't feeling that great. So Mom was on a liver transplant waiting list for 3 years and there were many close calls, and the only thing that kept her alive was the confessions of the Word of God over her life, healing scriptures and her trust in God. Finally she had her transplant and this year in September 2011 will be 3 years, so she is making up for lost time, gives God all the Glory and Praise, she gives testimony to others as much as she can.

My brother Junior married and has 3 children, He is a pastor of a church in Durango Mexico.

My sister Vanessa married and has 2 daughters, she lives in Colorado Springs.

My brother Lee has 3 boys and 1 girl, He lives in Phoenix Arizona.

My brother Alonso married and has a daughter and a brand new baby. He lives in New Mexico. He is a youth Pastor.

All of them are Rehma Graduates, we all love the lord and have a heart for him.

To me personally being a Christian is not about being fanatic, but far from it. It is about my walk with God in a daily basis, behind doors and out around others, it is the way I live. I aknowledge God in all I do. I hope to be a better person one day, but I know I will never be perfect. I will always have dreams and projects to dream about, that is what makes me who I am. I am a giver, I get the most pleasure from that and I know it is a gift from God.

Isaiah 66:2 I myself created the whole universe! I am pleased with those who are humble and repentant, who fear me and obey me,

Matthew 22:37-38 Jesus answered, "Love the Lord your God with all your heart, with all your soul, and with all your mind; this is the greatest and most important commandment.

It has been an honor for me to share part of my walk with God and I hope you can find joy and hope from these testimonies. We never leave our home without prayer in the mornings, covering ourselves with the Precious Blood of Jesus and speaking God's Divine protection over us and His Favor. We speak Godly order in our lives as well.

I believe God created us so that we could have a relationship with Him. He is pleased to see us enjoying life and being grateful about His Blessings.

Author's Biography

Born in 1964 in Durango, Mexico
To an American Father and a Mexican Mother

Lived in Australia for my first 5 ½ years

Moved back to Mexico to Durango

Then moved to the coast, Puerto Vallarta, Jalisco Mexico

Then eventually moved to New Mexico

Where I have lived for the last 31 years

In the Sangre de Cristo Mountains/The Rockies

My Father was born in Pearsall, Texas and his family moved when he was 2yrs

So he was raised in Durango, that being were my parents met

I met my husband when I was 21 years and we dated for 4 years and married 22 years in 2011.

Our Son will be 5 years in 2011

Our Dog Ruffie is 13 years and in great shape, we expect him to be with us for many, many more years to come!

Made in the USA
Middletown, DE
04 September 2023